'To the utterly
at-one with
Śiva there's
no dawn . . .'

D0595079

BASAVAṆṆA

MAHĀDĒVIYAKKA

ALLAMA PRABHU

Lived in the 12th century in what is now Karnataka, India

DĒVARA DĀSIMAYYA

Lived in the mid-10th century, probably in Mudanuru, India

Taken from A. K. Ramanujan's translation and edition of
Speaking of Śiva, first published in 1973.

Speaking of Śiva

Translated by
A. K. Ramanujan

PENGUIN BOOKS

PENGUIN CLASSICS

UK | USA | Canada | Ireland | Australia
India | New Zealand | South Africa

Penguin Books is part of the Penguin Random House group of companies
whose addresses can be found at global.penguinrandomhouse.com.

This selection published in Penguin Classics 2015
011

Translation copyright © A. K. Ramanujan 1973

Set in 9.5/13 pt Baskerville 10 Pro
Typeset by Jouve (UK), Milton Keynes
Printed and bound in Great Britain by Clays Ltd, Elcograf S.p.A.

A CIP catalogue record for this book is available from the British Library

ISBN: 978–0–141–39879–2

www.greenpenguin.co.uk

Contents

BASAVAṆṆA

Look, the world, in a swell
of waves, is beating upon my face.

Why should it rise to my heart,
tell me.
O tell me, why is it
rising now to my throat?
Lord,
how can I tell you anything
when it is risen high
over my head
lord lord
listen to my cries
O lord of the meeting rivers
listen.

Cripple me, father,
that I may not go here and there.
Blind me, father,
that I may not look at this and that.
Deafen me, father,
that I may not hear anything else.

Keep me
at your men's feet
looking for nothing else,
O lord of the meeting rivers.

Don't make me hear all day
    'Whose man, whose man, whose man is this?'

Let me hear, 'This man is mine, mine,
    this man is mine.'

O lord of the meeting rivers,
    make me feel I'm a son
    of the house.

Śiva, you have no mercy.
Śiva, you have no heart.

Why why did you bring me to birth,
    wretch in this world,
        exile from the other?

Tell me, lord,
don't you have one more
little tree or plant
made just for me?

As a mother runs
close behind her child
with his hand on a cobra
or a fire,

> the lord of the meeting rivers
> stays with me
> every step of the way
> and looks after me.

When a whore with a child
takes on a customer for money,

neither child nor lecher
will get enough of her.

She'll go pat the child once,
then go lie with the man once,

neither here nor there.
Love of money is relentless,

my lord of the meeting rivers.

A snake-charmer and his noseless wife,
snake in hand, walk carefully
trying to read omens
for a son's wedding,

but they meet head-on
a noseless woman
and her snake-charming husband,
and cry 'The omens are bad!'

His own wife has no nose;
there's a snake in his hand.
What shall I call such fools
who do not know themselves

and see only the others,

        O lord
        of the meeting
        rivers!

Before
   the grey reaches the cheek,
   the wrinkle the rounded chin
   and the body becomes a cage of bones:

before
   with fallen teeth
   and bent back
   you are someone else's ward:

before
   you drop your hand to the knee
   and clutch a staff:

before
   age corrodes
   your form:

before
   death touches you:

      worship
      our lord
      of the meeting rivers!

Make of my body the beam of a lute
    of my head the sounding gourd
    of my nerves the strings
    of my fingers the plucking rods.

Clutch me close
    and play your thirty-two songs
    O lord of the meeting rivers!

You went riding elephants.
You went riding horses.
You covered yourself
with vermilion and musk.

                  O brother,
but you went without the truth,
you went without sowing and reaping
the good.

         Riding rutting elephants
of pride, you turned easy target
to fate.

         You went without knowing
our lord of the meeting rivers.

You qualified for hell.

Look here, dear fellow:
I wear these men's clothes
only for you.

Sometimes I am man,
sometimes I am woman.

O lord of the meeting rivers
I'll make wars for you
but I'll be your devotees' bride.

The rich
will make temples for Śiva.
What shall I,
a poor man,
do?

My legs are pillars,
the body the shrine,
the head a cupola
of gold.

Listen, O lord of the meeting rivers,
things standing shall fall,
but the moving ever shall stay.

DĒVARA DĀSIMAYYA

You balanced the globe
    on the waters
    and kept it from melting away,

you made the sky stand
    without pillar or prop.

O Rāmanātha,
    which gods could have
    done this?

Dēvara Dāsimayya

A fire
in every act and look and word.
Between man and wife
a fire.
In the plate of food
eaten after much waiting
a fire.
In the loss of gain
a fire.
And in the infatuation
of coupling
a fire.

You have given us
five fires
and poured dirt in our mouths

O Rāmanātha.

The five elements
have become one.

The sun and the moon,
O Rider of the Bull,
aren't they really
your body?

I stand,
look on,
you're filled
with the worlds.

What can I hurt now
after this, Rāmanātha?

Whatever It was

that made this earth
the base,
the world its life,
the wind its pillar,
arranged the lotus and the moon,
and covered it all with folds
of sky

with Itself inside,

to that Mystery
indifferent to differences,

to It I pray,
O Rāmanātha.

What does it matter
if the fox roams
all over the Jambu island?
Will he ever stand amazed
in meditation of the Lord?
Does it matter if he wanders
all over the globe
and bathes in a million sacred rivers?

A pilgrim who's not one with you,
Rāmanātha,
roams the world
like a circus man.

To the utterly at-one with Śiva

there's no dawn,
no new moon,
no noonday,
nor equinoxes,
nor sunsets,
nor full moons;

his front yard
is the true Benares,

O Rāmanātha.

If they see
breasts and long hair coming
they call it woman,

if beard and whiskers
they call it man:

but, look, the self that hovers
in between
is neither man
nor woman

O Rāmanātha.

Suppose you cut a tall bamboo
in two;
make the bottom piece a woman,
the headpiece a man;
rub them together
till they kindle:

      tell me now,
the fire that's born,
is it male or female,

      O Rāmanātha?

MAHĀDĒVIYAKKA

You're like milk
in water: I cannot tell
what comes before,
what after;
which is the master,
which the slave;
what's big,
what's small.

O lord white as jasmine
if an ant should love you
and praise you,
will he not grow
to demon powers?

Illusion has troubled body as shadow
    troubled life as a heart
    troubled heart as a memory
    troubled memory as awareness.

With stick raised high, Illusion herds
    the worlds.
    Lord white as jasmine
    no one can overcome
    your Illusion.

It was like a stream
   running into the dry bed
   of a lake,
        like rain
pouring on plants
parched to sticks.

It was like this world's pleasure
   and the way to the other,
                 both
   walking towards me.

Seeing the feet of the master,
O lord white as jasmine,
   I was made
   worthwhile.

When I didn't know myself
where were you?

Like the colour in the gold,
you were in me.

I saw in you,
lord white as jasmine,
the paradox of your being
in me
without showing a limb.

Locks of shining red hair
a crown of diamonds
small beautiful teeth
and eyes in a laughing face
that light up fourteen worlds –
  I saw His glory,
and seeing, I quell today
the famine in my eyes.

I saw the haughty Master
for whom men, all men,
are but women, wives.

I saw the Great One
who plays at love
with Śakti,
original to the world,

I saw His stance
and began to live.

Four parts of the day
I grieve for you.
Four parts of the night
I'm mad for you.

I lie lost
sick for you, night and day,
   O lord white as jasmine.

Since your love
was planted,
I've forgotten hunger,
thirst, and sleep.

Listen, sister, listen.
I had a dream

I saw rice, betel, palmleaf
and coconut.
I saw an ascetic
come to beg,
white teeth and small matted curls.

I followed on his heels
and held his hand,
he who goes breaking
all bounds and beyond.

I saw the lord, white as jasmine,
and woke wide open.

When one heart touches
    and feels another
won't feeling weigh over all,
can it stand any decencies then?

O mother, you must be crazy,
I fell for my lord
    white as jasmine,
I've given in utterly.

Go, go, I'll have nothing
of your mother-and-daughter stuff.
You go now.

Husband inside,
lover outside.
I can't manage them both.

This world
and that other,
I cannot manage them both.

O lord white as jasmine

I cannot hold in one hand
both the round nut
and the long bow.

Why do I need this dummy
    of a dying world?
    illusion's chamberpot,
    hasty passions' whorehouse,
    this crackpot
    and leaky basement?

Finger may squeeze the fig
    to feel it, yet not choose
    to eat it.

Take me, flaws and all,
O lord

white as jasmine.

I love the Handsome One:
    he has no death
    decay nor form
    no place or side
    no end nor birthmarks.
    I love him O mother. Listen.

I love the Beautiful One
    with no bond nor fear
    no clan no land
    no landmarks
    for his beauty.

So my lord, white as jasmine, is my husband.

Take these husbands who die,
    decay, and feed them
    to your kitchen fires!

Riding the blue sapphire mountains
wearing moonstone for slippers
blowing long horns
O Śiva
when shall I
crush you on my pitcher breasts

O lord white as jasmine
when do I join you
stripped of body's shame
and heart's modesty?

What do
the barren know
of birthpangs?

Stepmothers,
what do they know
of loving care?

How can the unwounded
know the pain
of the wounded?

O lord white as jasmine
your love's blade stabbed
and broken in my flesh,

I writhe.
O mothers
how can you know me?

The heart in misery
has turned
upside down.

> The blowing gentle breeze
> is on fire.
> O friend moonlight burns
> like the sun.

Like a tax-collector in a town
I go restlessly here and there.

> Dear girl go tell Him
> bring Him to His senses.
> Bring Him back.

My lord white as jasmine
is angry
that we are two.

ALLAMA PRABHU

I saw:
    heart conceive,
      hand grow big with child;
    ear drink up the smell
        of camphor, nose eat up
    the dazzle of pearls;
      hungry eyes devour
    diamonds.
         In a blue sapphire
    I saw the three worlds
      hiding,
        O Lord of Caves.

If mountains shiver in the cold
with what
will they wrap them?

If space goes naked
with what
shall they clothe it?

If the lord's men become worldlings
where will I find the metaphor,

    O Lord of Caves.

Before anyone calls him, he calls them.
I saw him clamber over the forehead of the wild
elephant
born in his womb
and sway in play
in the dust of the winds.

I saw him juggle his body as a ball
in the depth of the sky,
play with a ten-hooded snake
in a basket; saw him blindfold
the eyes of the five virgins.
I saw him trample the forehead
of the lion that wanders in the ten streets,
I saw him raise the lion's eyebrows.
I saw him grow from amazement
to amazement, holding a diamond
in his hand.

       Nothing added,
nothing taken,

          the Lord's stance
          is invisible
          to men untouched
          by the Liṅga of the Breath.

A wilderness grew
in the sky.
In that wilderness
a hunter.
In the hunter's hands
a deer.

> The hunter will not die
> till the beast
> is killed.

Awareness is not easy,
is it,
O Lord of Caves?

For a wedding of dwarfs
rascals beat the drums
and whores
carry on their heads
holy pitchers;

> with hey-ho's and loud hurrahs
> they crowd the wedding party
> and quarrel over flowers and betelnuts;

> all three worlds are at the party;
> what a rumpus this is,
> without our Lord of Caves.

The fires of the city burned in the forest,
forest fires burned in the town.
Listen, listen to the flames
of the four directions.
Flapping and crackling in the vision
a thousand bodies dance in it
and die countless deaths,

O Lord of Caves.

If it rains fire
    you have to be as the water;

if it is a deluge of water
    you have to be as the wind;

if it is the Great Flood,
    you have to be as the sky;

and if it is the Very Last Flood of all the worlds,
    you have to give up self

and become the Lord.

Who can know green grass flames
    seeds of stone

    reflections of water
    smell of the wind

    the sap of fire
    the taste of sunshine on the tongue

    and the lights in oneself

except your men?

One dies,
another bears him to the burial ground:
still another takes them both
and burns them.

No one knows the groom
and no one the bride.
Death falls across
the wedding.

Much before the decorations fade
the bridegroom is dead.

Lord, only your men
have no death.

The wind sleeps
to lullabies of sky.

Space drowses,
infinity gives it suck
from her breast.

The sky is silent.
The lullaby is over.

The Lord is
as if He were not.

Light
devoured darkness.

I was alone
inside.

Shedding
the visible dark

I
was Your target

O Lord of Caves.

Sleep, great goddess sleep,
heroine of three worlds,
spins and sucks up
    all, draws breath
    and throws them down
    sapless.

I know of no hero
    who can stand before her.
    Struck by her arrows,
    people rise and fall.

Some say
they saw It.
What is It,
the circular sun,
the circle of the stars?

The Lord of Caves
lives in the town
of the moon mountain.

Allama Prabhu

Looking for your light,
I went out:

> it was like the sudden dawn
> of a million million suns,

> a ganglion of lightnings
> for my wonder.

> O Lord of Caves,
> if you are light,
> there can be no metaphor.